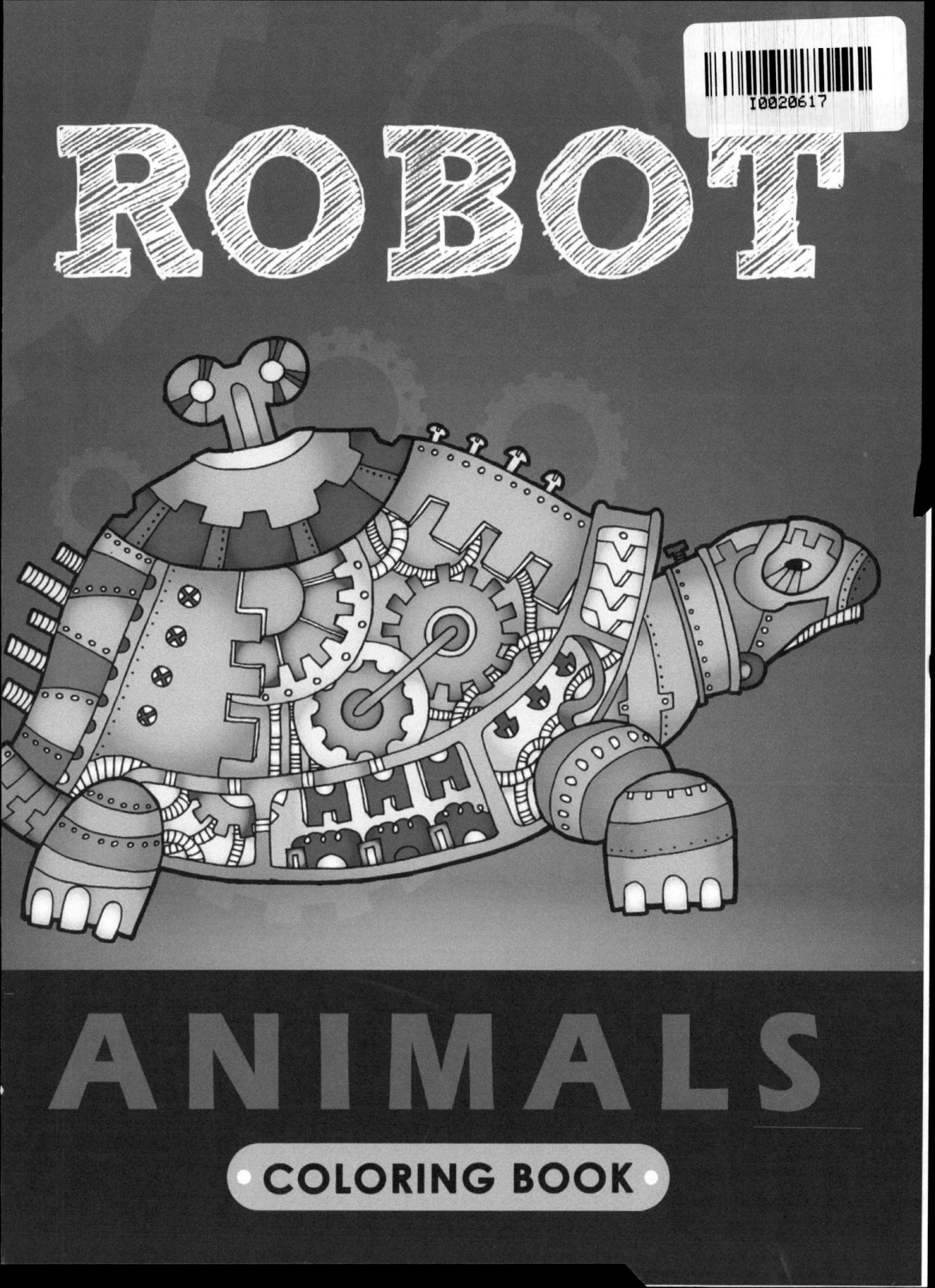

PUBLISHED IN 2018 BY
KODOMO PUBLISHING

COPYRIGHT 'ILLUSTRATIONS' 2018 KODOMO PUBLISHING
ALL RIGHT RESERVED. 'NO PART OF THIS PUBLICATION MAY BE REPORDICED OR TRANSMITTED IN ANY FORM OR BY ANY MEANS. ELECTRONIC, OR MECHANICAL,INCLUDING PHOTOCOPY, RECORDING OR ANY INFORMATION STORAGE SYSTEM AND RETRIEVAL SYSTEM WITHOUT PERMISSION IN WRITING BY PUBLISHER 'KODOMO PUBLISHING'

PRINTED IN THE UNITED STATES OF AMERICA

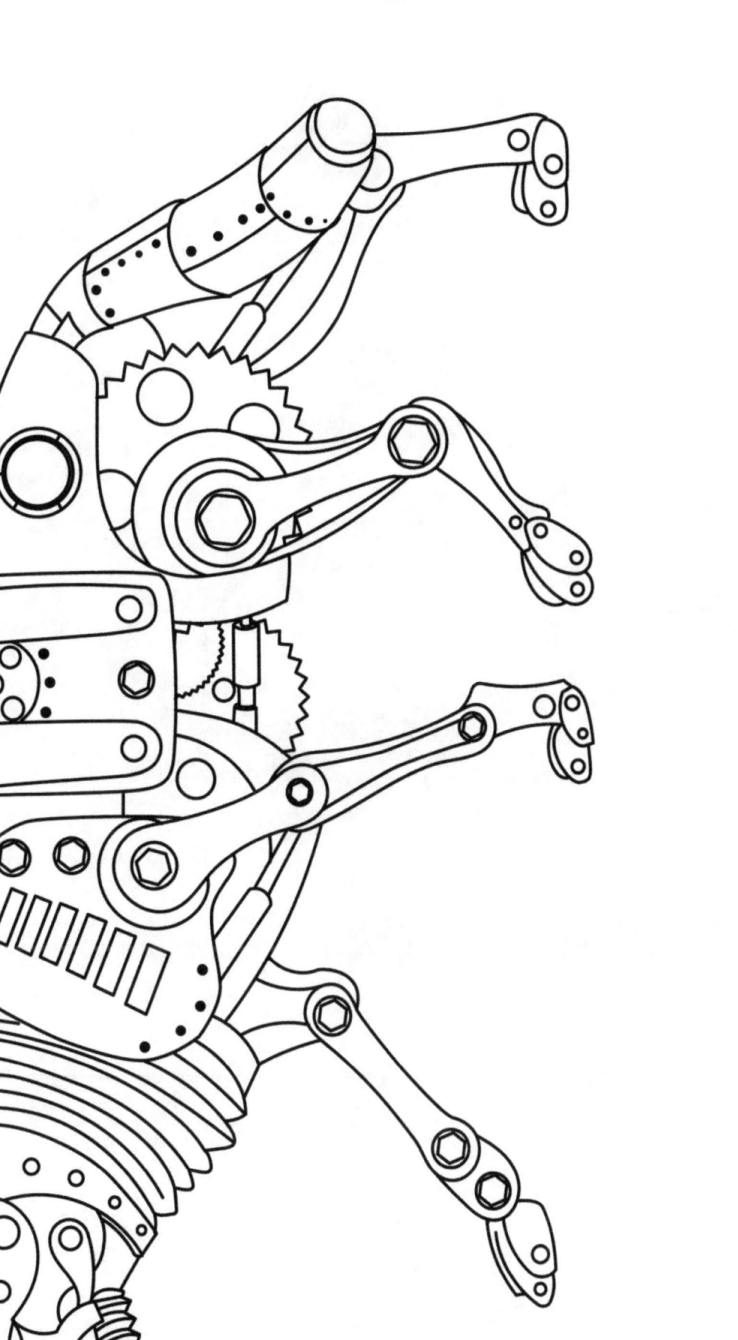

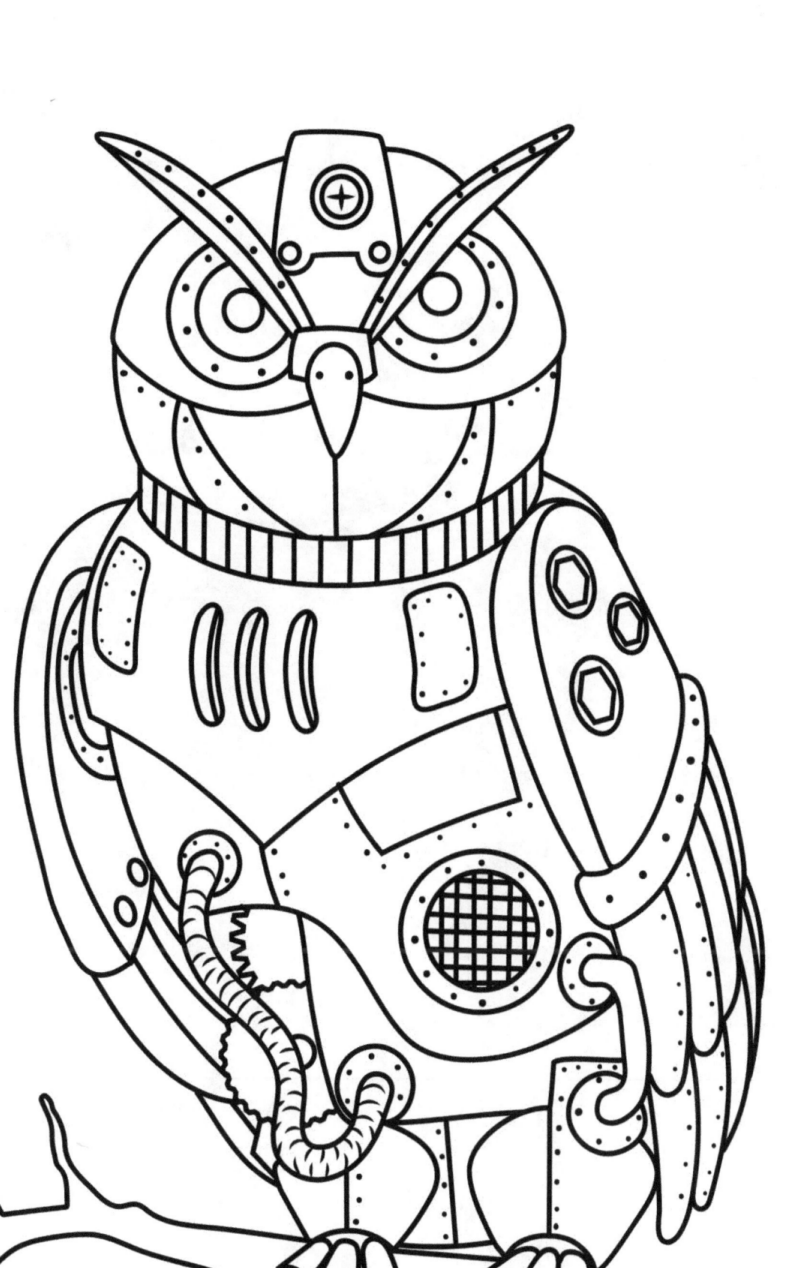

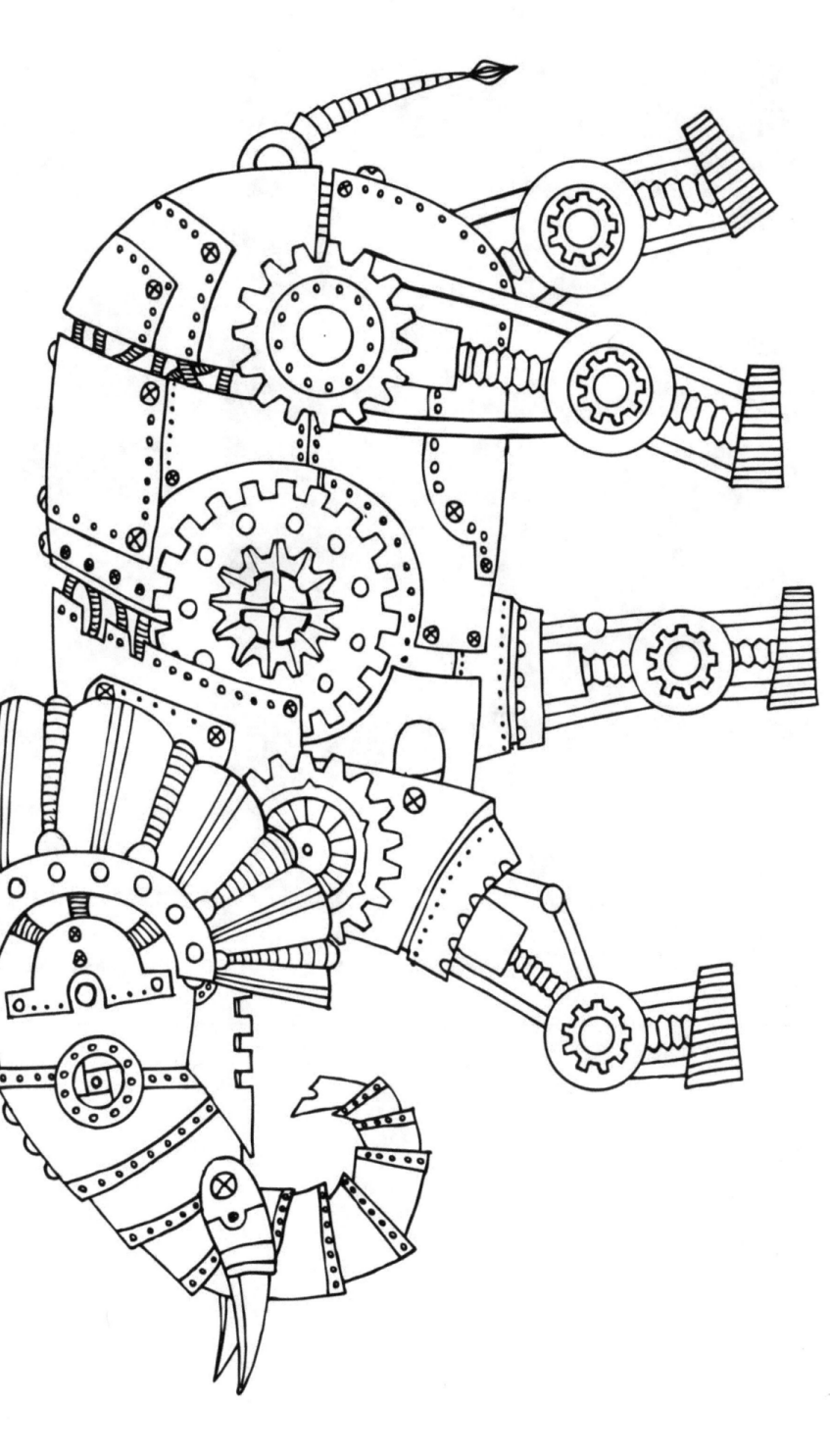

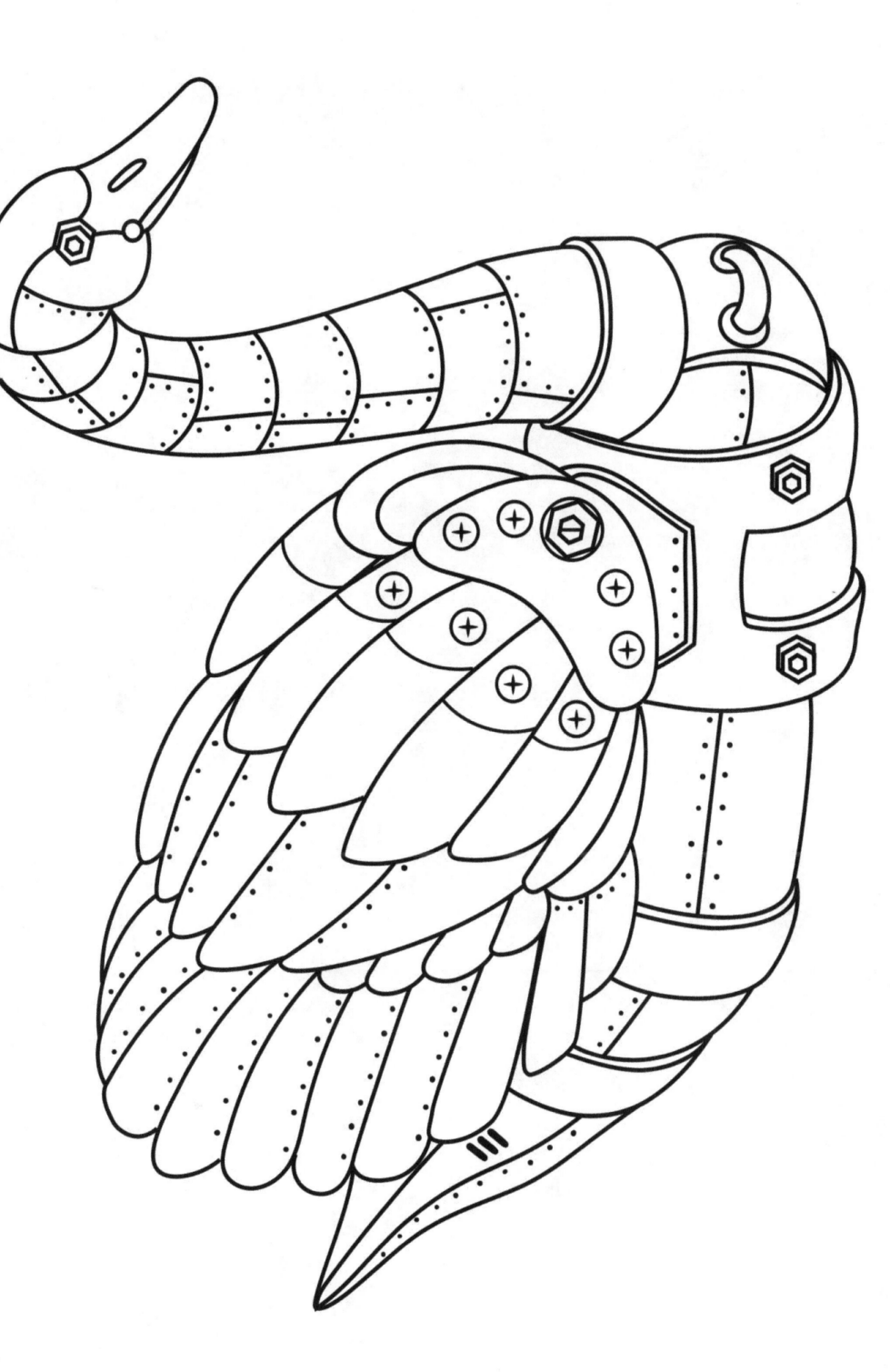

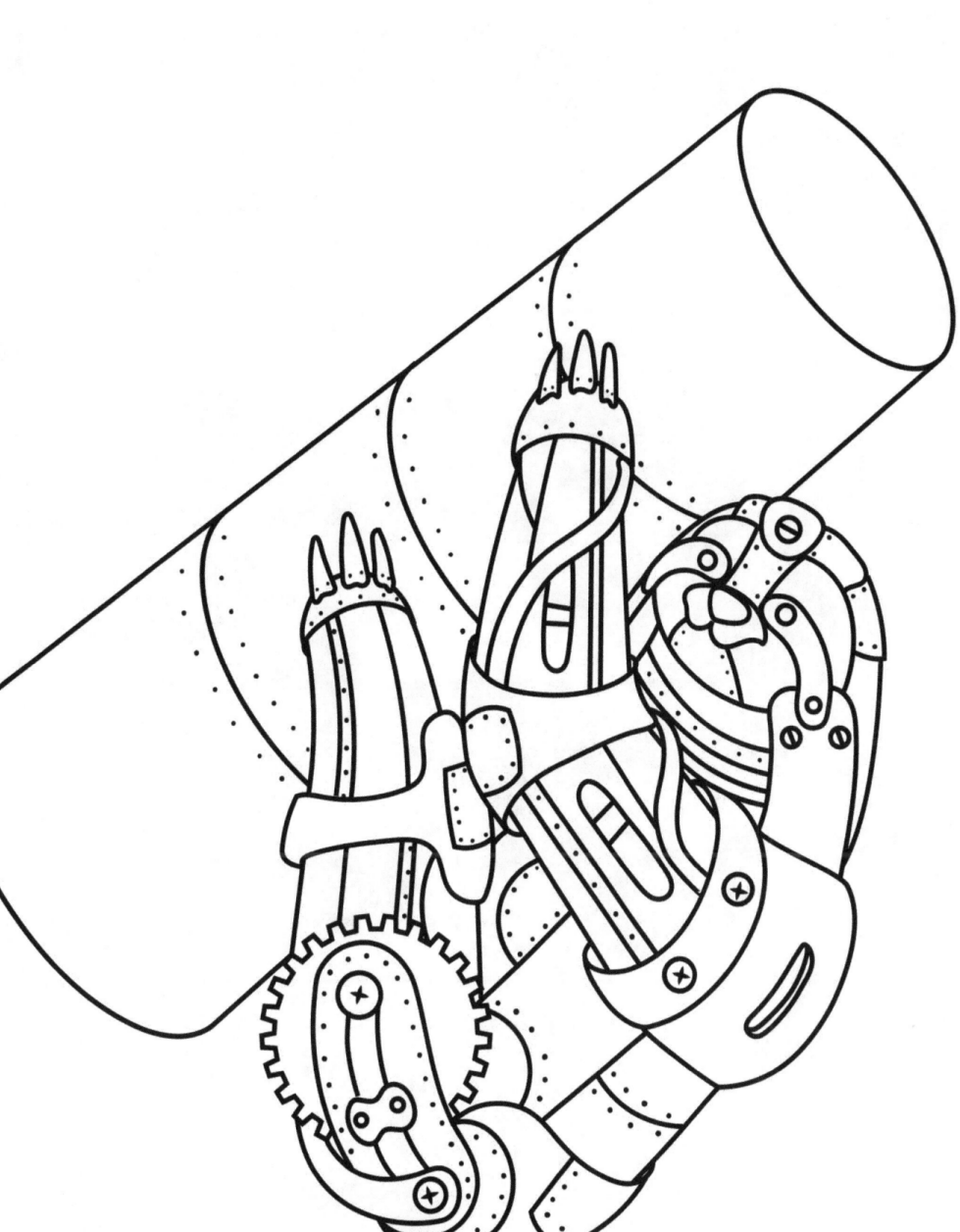

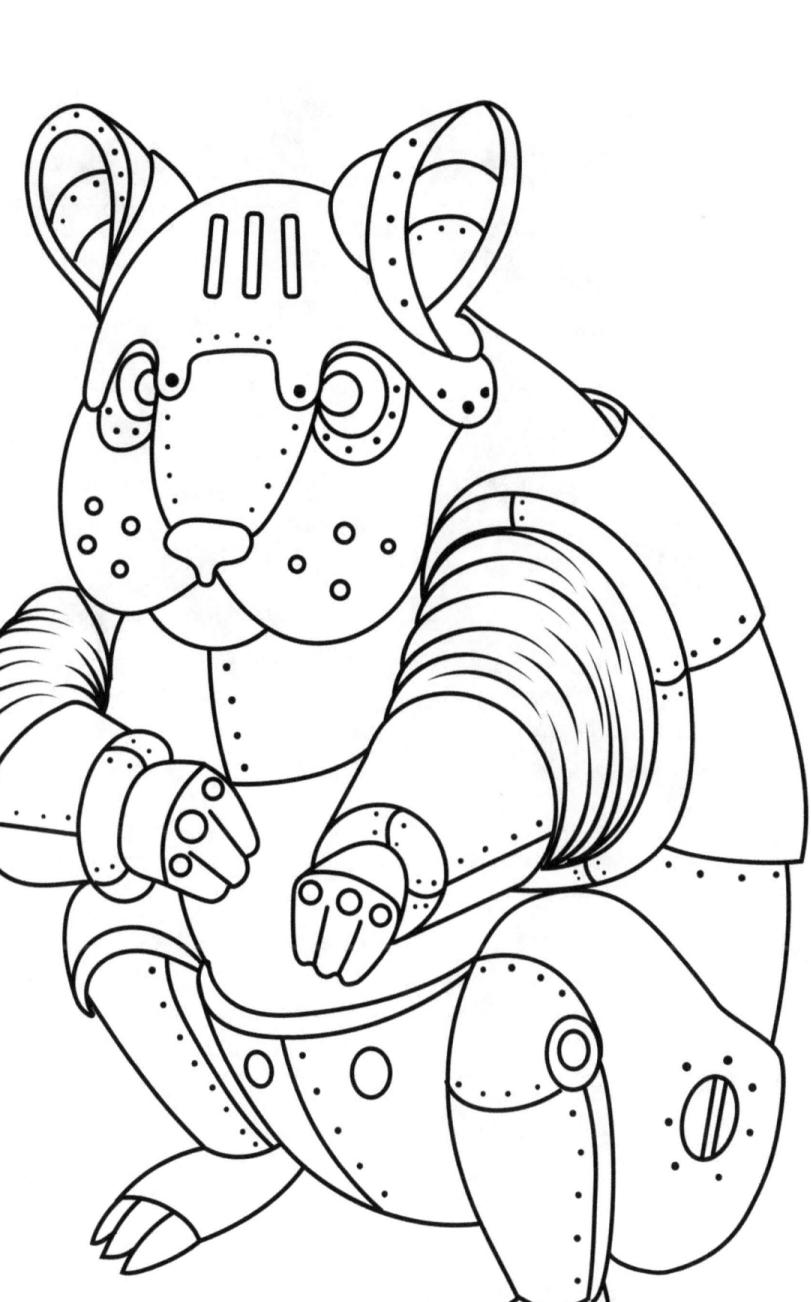

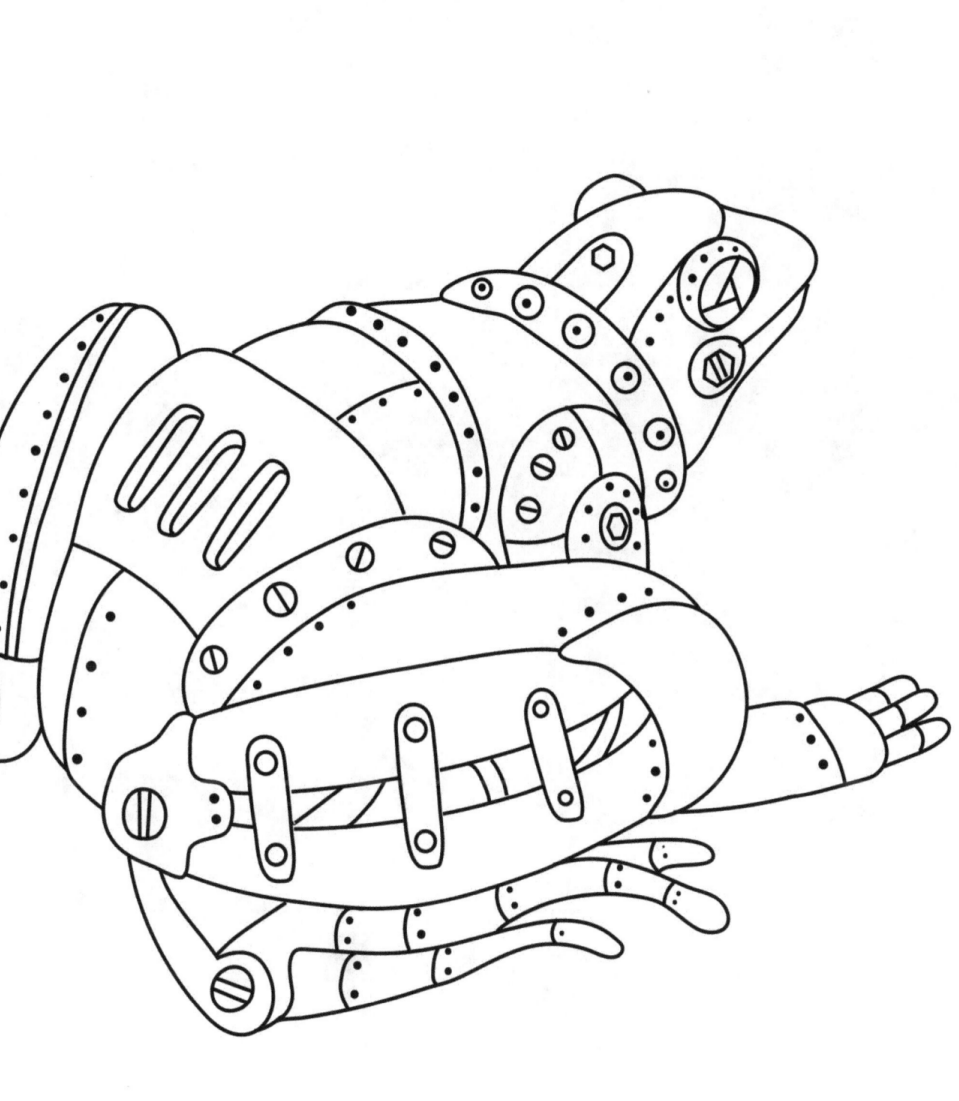

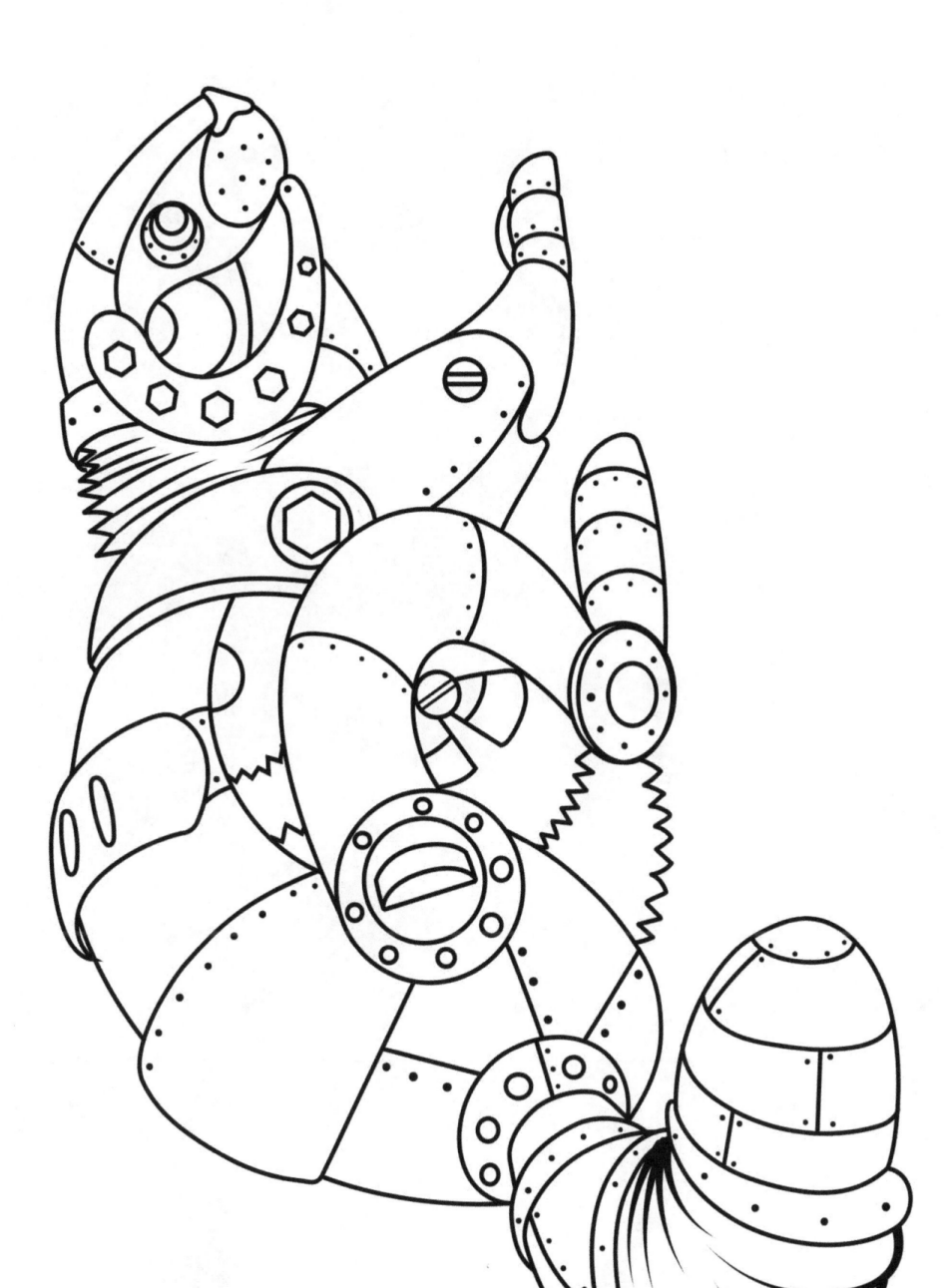

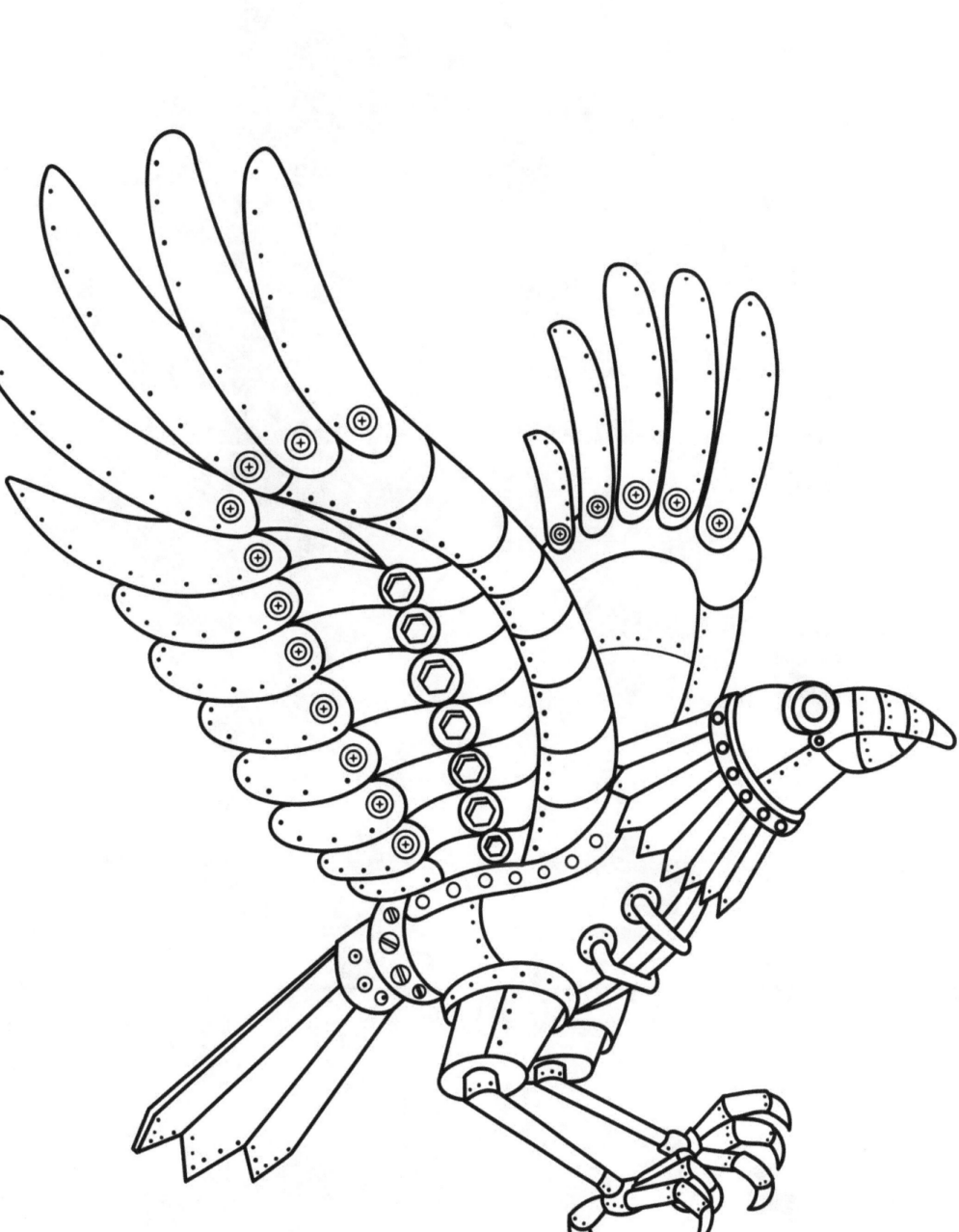

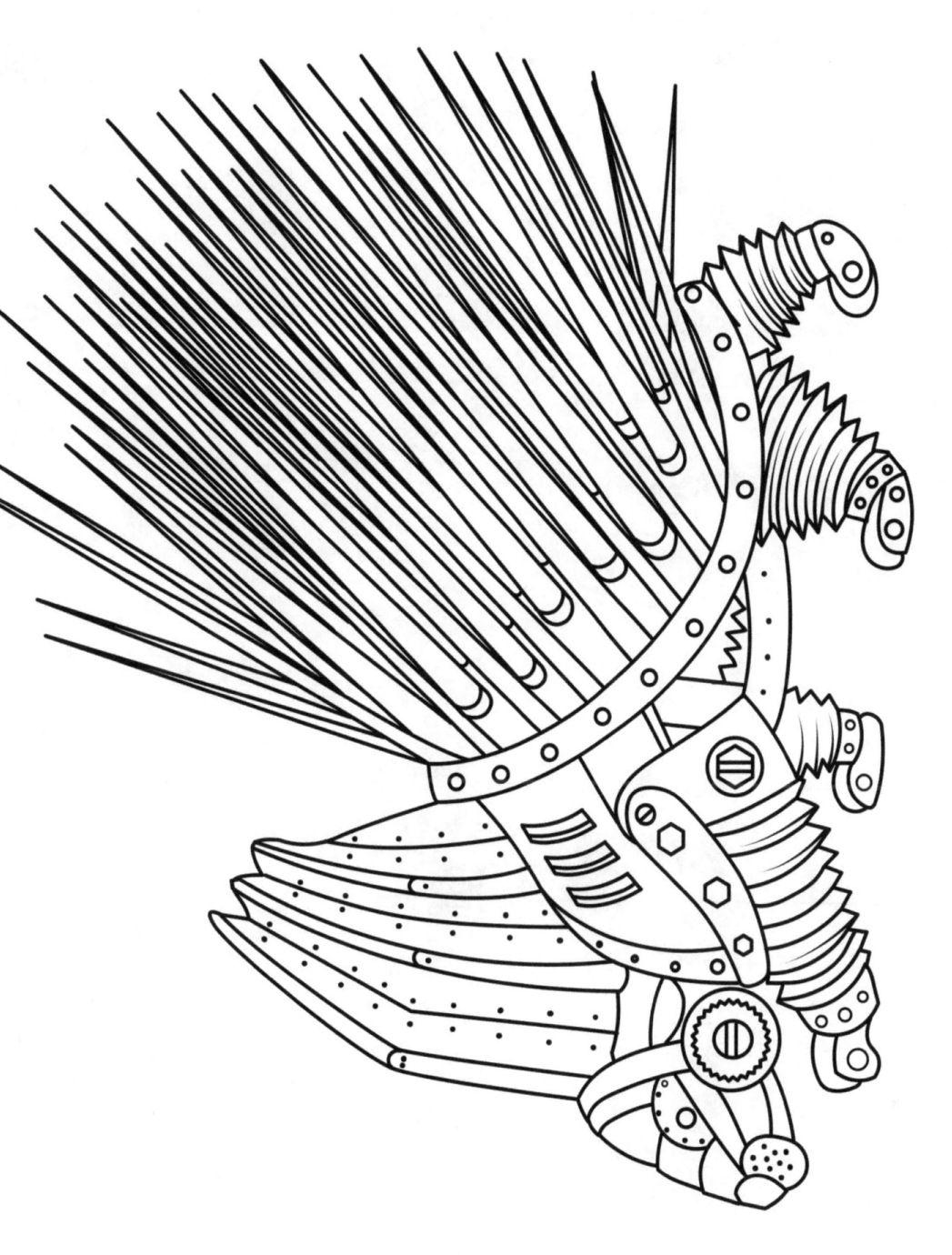

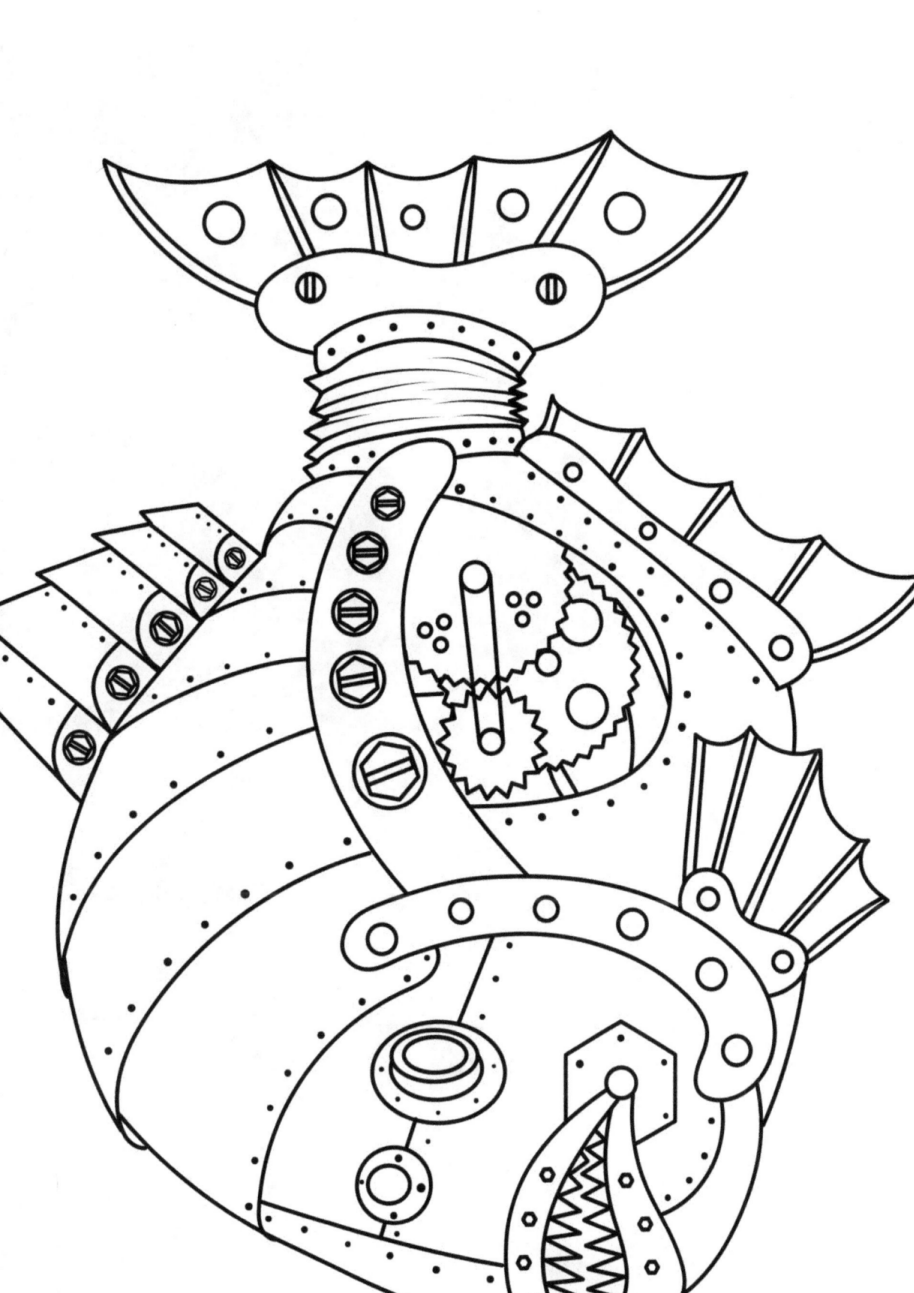

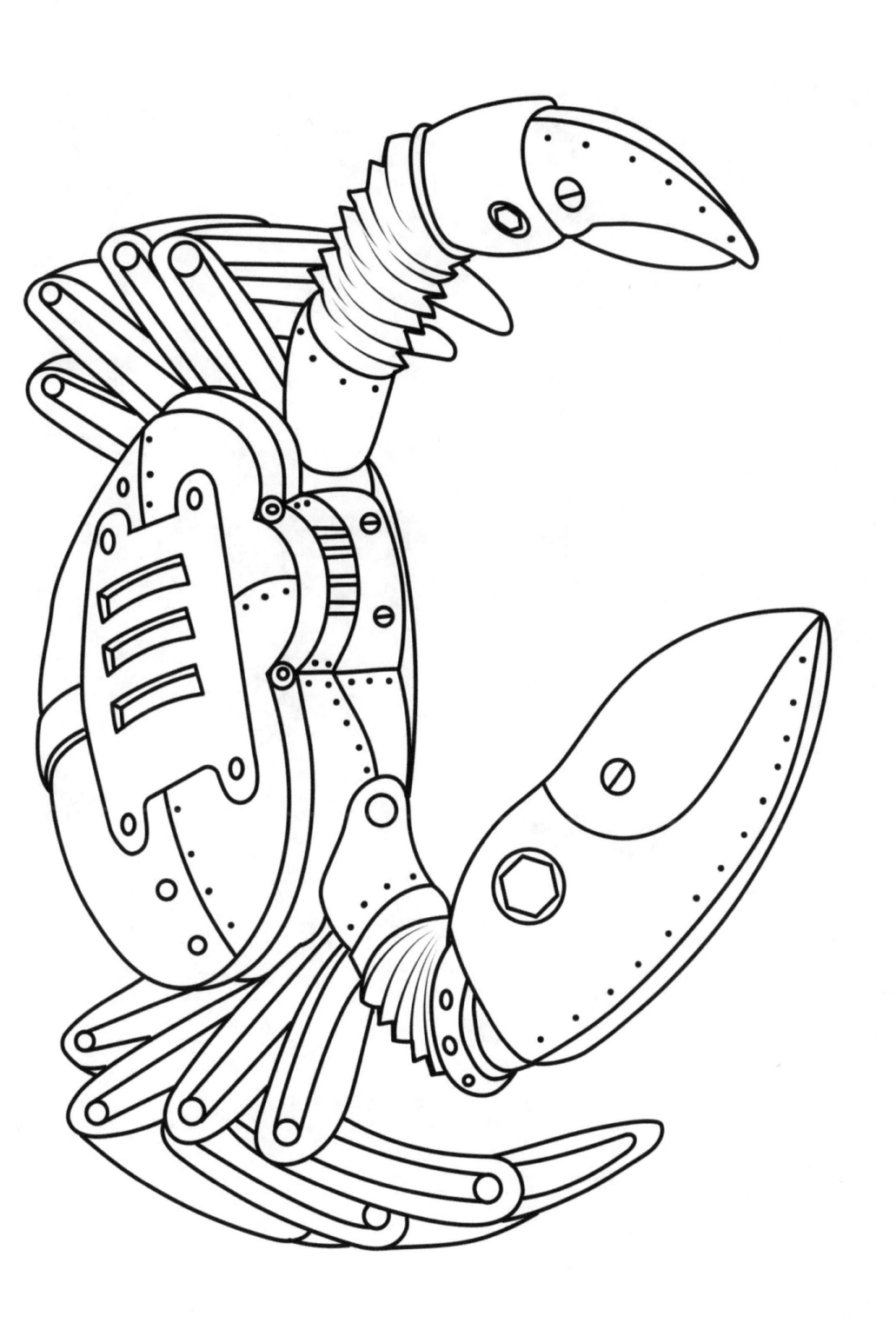

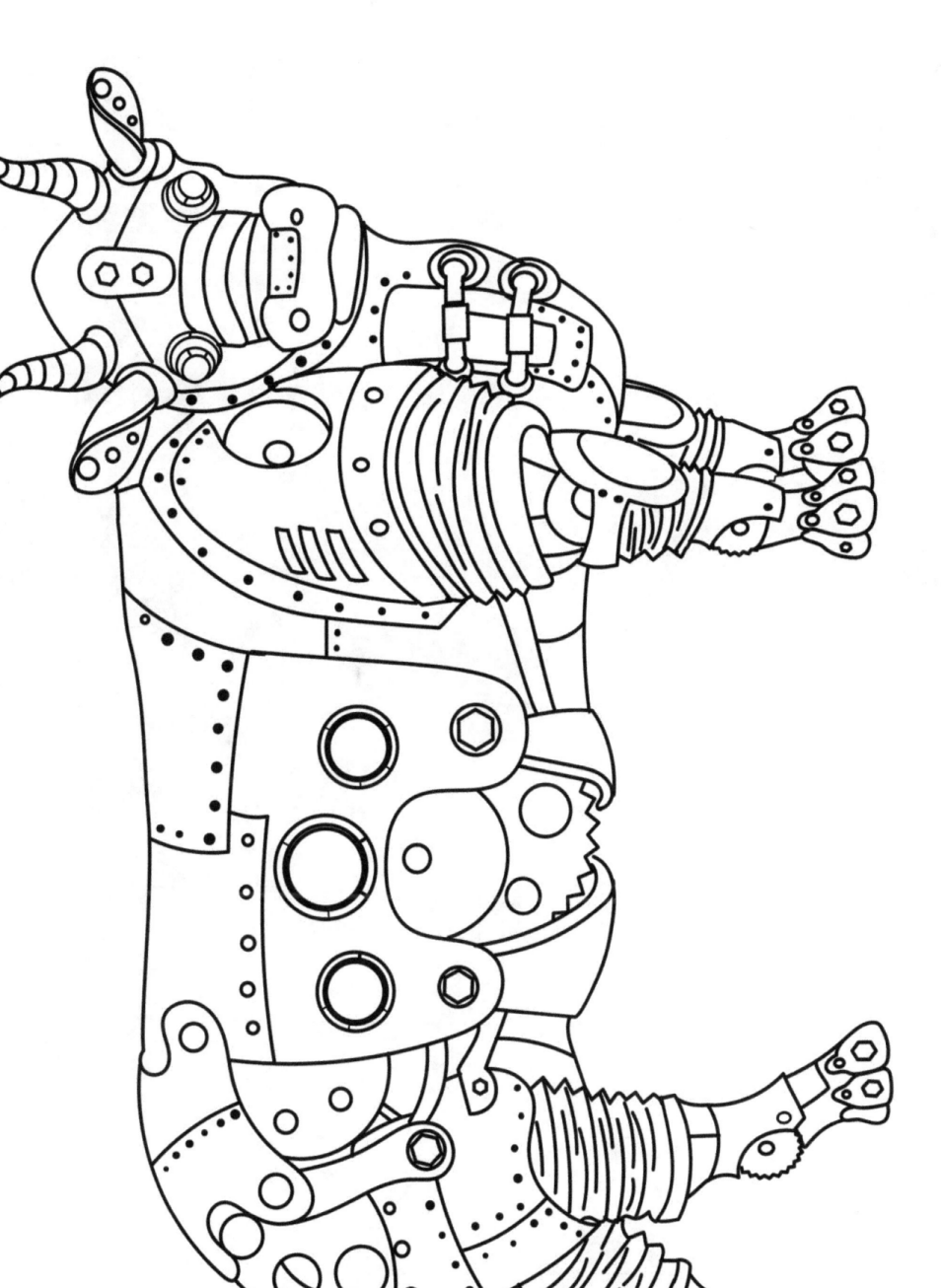

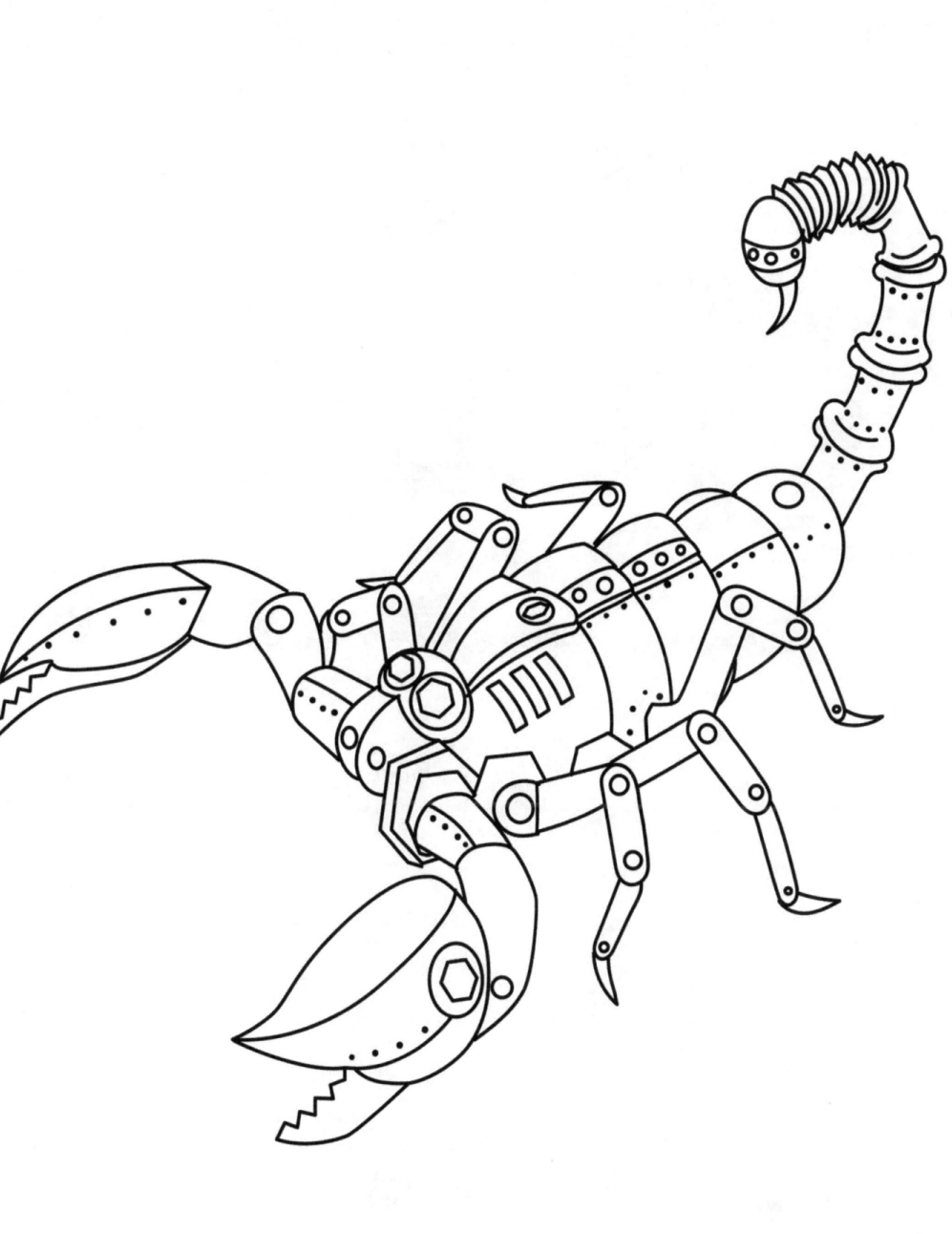

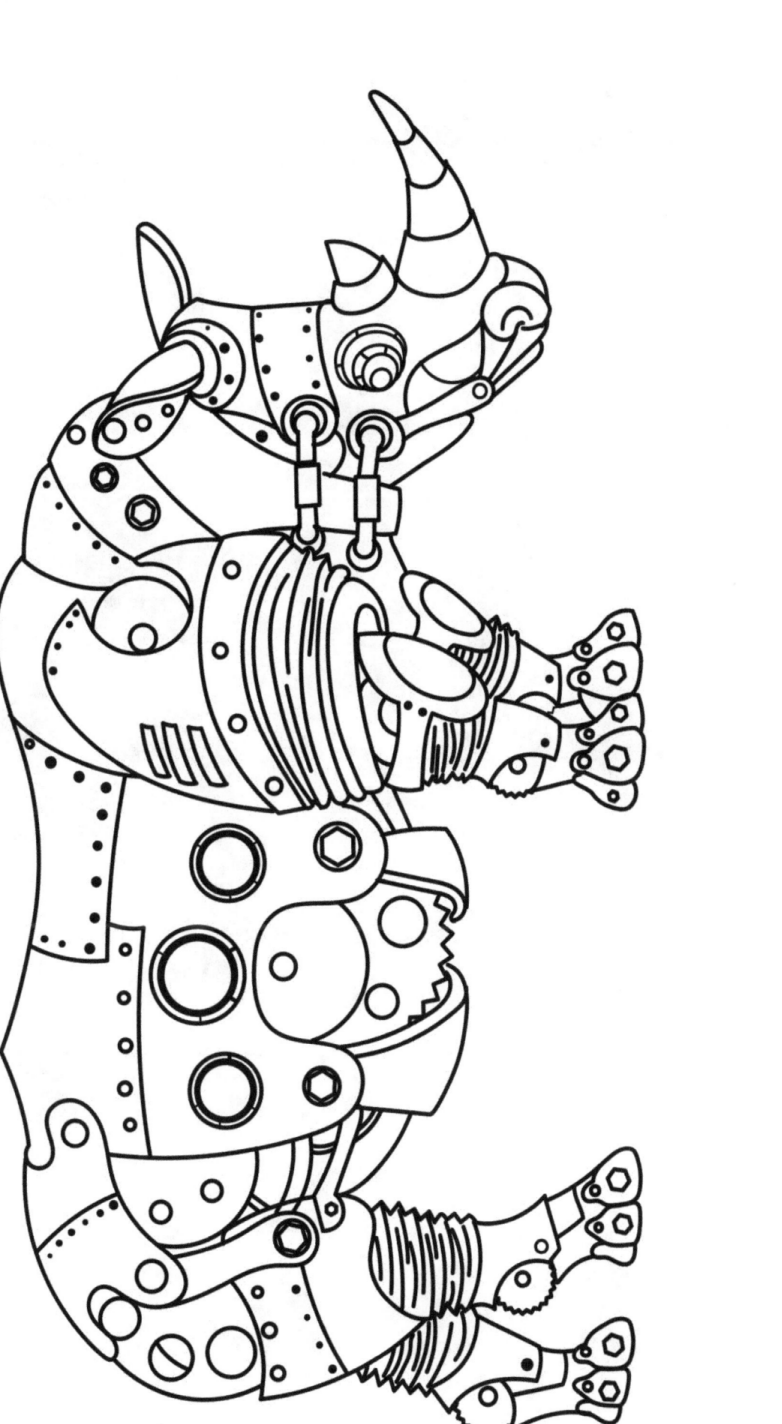